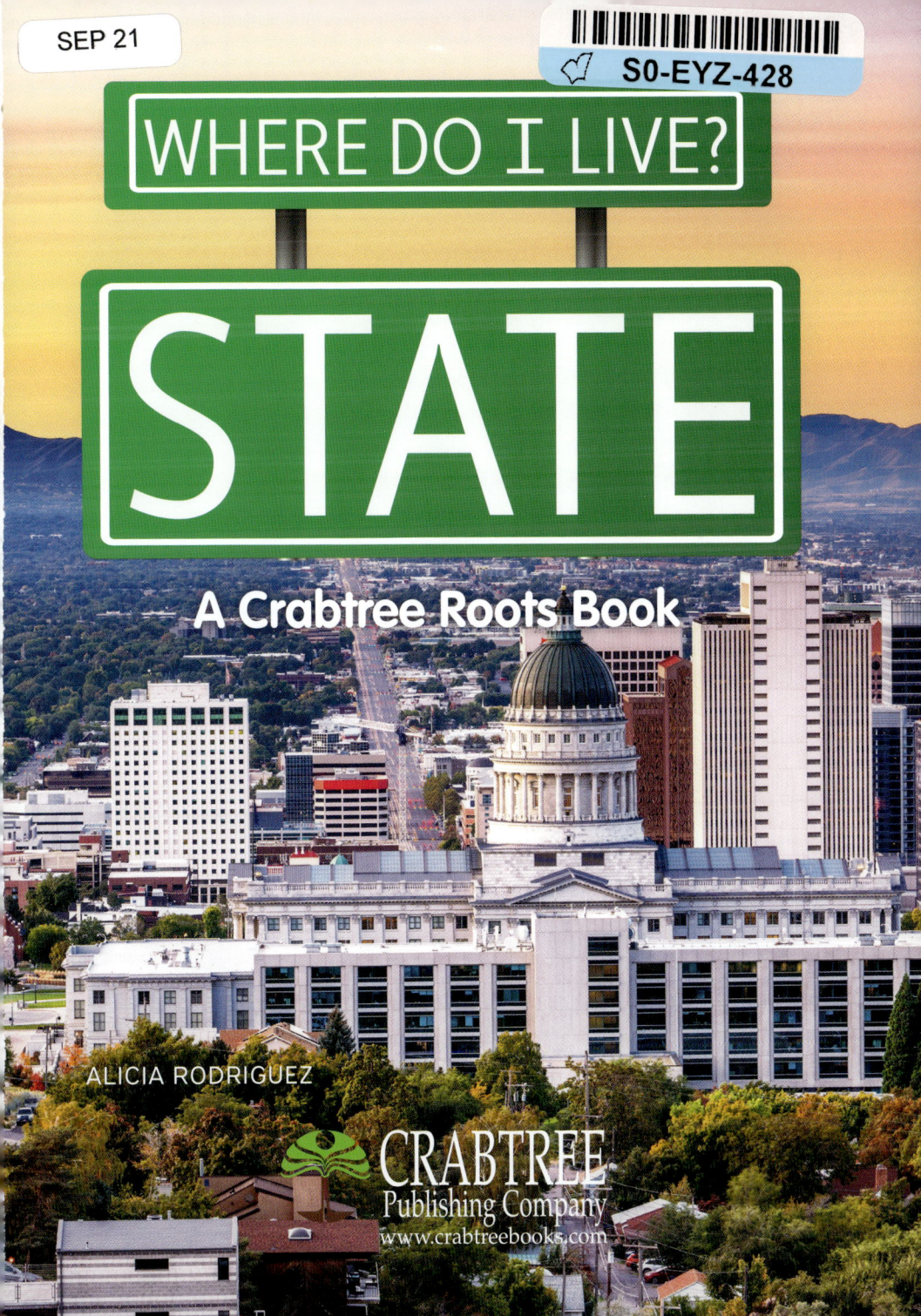

WHERE DO I LIVE?
STATE

A Crabtree Roots Book

ALICIA RODRIGUEZ

CRABTREE
Publishing Company
www.crabtreebooks.com

School-to-Home Support for Caregivers and Teachers

This book helps children grow by letting them practice reading. Here are a few guiding questions to help the reader with building his or her comprehension skills. Possible answers appear here in red.

Before Reading:
- What do I think this book is about?
    - *I think this book is about what a state looks like.*
    - *I think this book is about what you can find in a state.*
- What do I want to learn about this topic?
    - *I want to learn how big a state is.*
    - *I want to learn who runs a state.*

During Reading:
- I wonder why...
    - *I wonder why a state has its own flag.*
    - *I wonder why a country can be made up of states.*
- What have I learned so far?
    - *I have learned that the governor is the leader of a state.*
    - *I have learned that some states have beaches.*

After Reading:
- What details did I learn about this topic?
    - *I have learned that states can be different shapes and sizes.*
    - *I have learned that states have leaders.*
- Read the book again and look for the vocabulary words.
    - *I see the word **state** on page 3 and the word **flags** on page 10. The other vocabulary words are found on page 14.*

I live in a **state.**

It is part of a **country**.

United States of America

The **governor** is the leader.

Some states have **beaches**.

Some states have **mountains**.

All states have **flags**.

What state do you live in?

Word List
Sight Words

a	in	some
all	is	the
do	it	what
have	live	you
I	of	

Words to Know

beaches

country

flags

governor

mountains

state

34 Words

I live in a **state**.

It is part of a **country**.

The **governor** is the leader.

Some states have **beaches**.

Some states have **mountains**.

All states have **flags**.

What state do you live in?

Written by: Alicia Rodriguez
Designed by: Rhea Wallace
Series Development: James Earley
Proofreader: Janine Deschenes
Educational Consultant: Marie Lemke M.Ed.

Photographs:
Shutterstock: Alex Stiop: cover; Sean Pavone:
    p. 1, 12; Kevin Ruck: p. 3, 14; El Nariz: p. 7, 14;
    TierneyMJ: p. 8, 14; Lillac: p. 9, 14; BoxLab:
    p. 11, 14

Library and Archives Canada Cataloguing in Publication
Title: State / Alicia Rodriguez.
Names: Rodriguez, Alicia (Children's author), author.
Description: Series statement: Where do I live? |
    "A Crabtree roots book".
Identifiers: Canadiana (print) 20210182911 |
    Canadiana (ebook) 2021018292X |
    ISBN 9781427160010 (hardcover) |
    ISBN 9781427160072 (softcover) |
    ISBN 9781427133632 (HTML) |
    ISBN 9781427134233 (EPUB) |
    ISBN 9781427160256 (read-along ebook)
Subjects: LCSH: U.S. states—Juvenile literature.
Classification: LCC E180 .R63 2022 | DDC j973—dc23

Library of Congress Cataloging-in-Publication Data
Names: Rodriguez, Alicia (Children's author), author.
Title: State / Alicia Rodriguez.
Description: New York, NY : Crabtree Publishing Company,
    [2022] | Series: Where do I live? | "A Crabtree roots book."
Identifiers: LCCN 2021015108 (print) |
    LCCN 2021015109 (ebook) |
    ISBN 9781427160010 (hardcover) |
    ISBN 9781427160072 (paperback) |
    ISBN 9781427133632 (ebook) |
    ISBN 9781427134233 (epub) |
    ISBN 9781427160256
Subjects: LCSH: U.S. states--Juvenile literature.
Classification: LCC E180 .R63 2022 (print) | LCC E180 (ebook)
    | DDC 973--dc23
LC record available at https://lccn.loc.gov/2021015108
LC ebook record available at https://lccn.loc.gov/2021015109

Crabtree Publishing Company

www.crabtreebooks.com   1-800-387-7650

Printed in the U.S.A./062021/CG20210401

Copyright © 2022 **CRABTREE PUBLISHING COMPANY**

All rights reserved. No part of this publication may be reproduced, stored in a retrieval system or be transmitted in any form or by any means, electronic, mechanical, photocopying, recording, or otherwise, without the prior written permission of Crabtree Publishing Company. In Canada: We acknowledge the financial support of the Government of Canada through the Canada Book Fund for our publishing activities.

Published in the United States
Crabtree Publishing
347 Fifth Avenue, Suite 1402-145
New York, NY, 10016

Published in Canada
Crabtree Publishing
616 Welland Ave.
St. Catharines, Ontario L2M 5V6